WE BUILT THIS CITY

PHILADELPHIA

History, People, Landmarks

INDEPENDENCE HALL • TROLLEYS • THE ROCKY STATUE

PHILIP WOLNY

Paperback ISBN 979-8-89094-052-0
Hardcover ISBN 979-8-89094-053-7

Library of Congress Control Number: 2023943823

To learn more about the other great books from Fox Chapel Publishing, or to find a retailer near you, call toll-free 800-457-9112 or visit us at *www.FoxChapelPublishing.com*.

We are always looking for talented authors. To submit an idea, please send a brief inquiry to acquisitions@foxchapelpublishing.com.

Fox Chapel Publishing makes every effort to use environmentally friendly paper for printing.

Printed in China

ABOUT THE AUTHOR: Philip Wolny was born in Poland, but has lived in the United States since the age of four. He is an author and editor, whose nonfiction titles for young-adult readers include books about U.S history, international politics, geographic locations such as Los Angeles and Delaware, culture, religion, and many other topics. He lives with his wife and daughter in New York City.

PHILADELPHIA

 Philadelphia, Pennsylvania

 6th largest city in the USA

 141.7 square miles

 Population: 1.58 million

 Elevation: 39 ft.

 Settled: 1682

Philadelphia
is the birthplace of
the United States

Philadelphia stands as an iconic cornerstone of the nation's history and a testament to the country's diversity. From Independence Hall, where the Declaration of Independence and the United States Constitution were painstakingly forged, to the cobblestone streets of Old City, visitors can walk in the footsteps of the Founding Fathers. Philadelphia is also a modern hub of education, innovation, and diversity. The city is home to many institutions of higher learning, including Ivy League University of Pennsylvania, and to a rich array of neighborhoods and cultural communities. Explore the heart of the iconic City of Brotherly Love. Welcome to Philadelphia!

CONTENTS

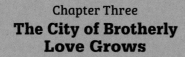

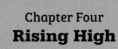

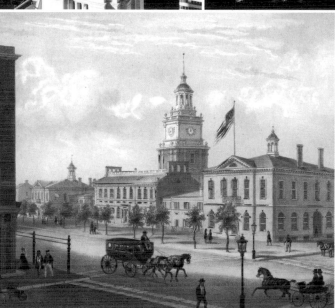

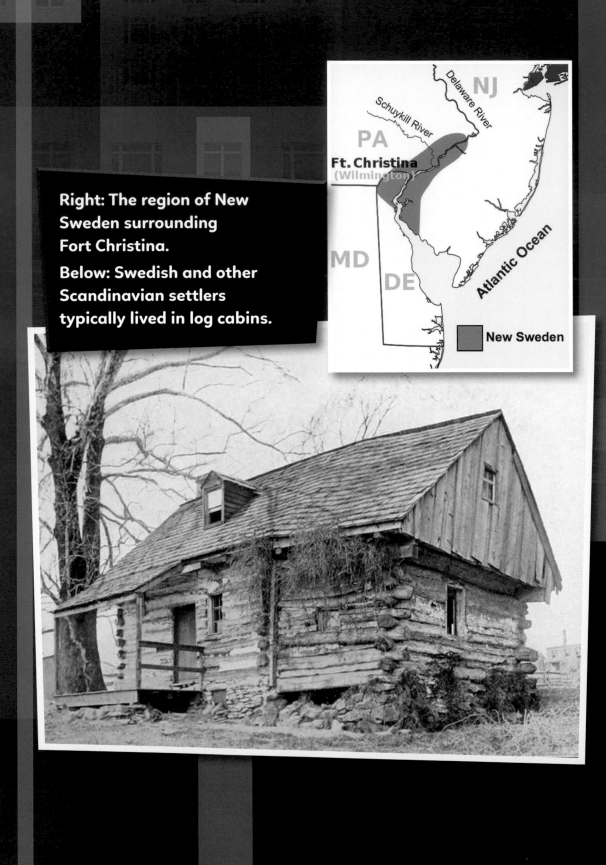

Right: The region of New Sweden surrounding Fort Christina.

Below: Swedish and other Scandinavian settlers typically lived in log cabins.

NJ

Schuykill River

Delaware River

PA

Ft. Christina
(Wilmington)

MD

DE

Atlantic Ocean

New Sweden

New Sweden, New World

Imagine waking up in a log cabin overlooking the Delaware River, in a place called New Sweden. It's a busy day for you and your parents if you are one of the handful of Swedes, Dutch, and Finns who make their home here. Not too far away, you have neighbors—not Europeans, but the local Lenape who sometimes trade with the townspeople. Instead of the bold skyline of modern Philadelphia, the city's many neighborhoods, or its sports stadiums, it is wilderness as far as the eye can see. The Swedes settled in the Delaware River Valley in 1638. With other Scandinavians, they were likely among the first to actually build log cabins, bringing that tradition from their homelands.

In the beginning, the Lenape, Swedes, and Dutch and English traders lived together peacefully. Every year, the Swedes gave the Native Americans gifts for letting them live there. It seemed the least they could do, since the Lenape had occupied the area for nearly 10,000 years.

The growing colony came into conflict with a much bigger power: Dutch settlers, led by Peter Stuyvesant, who ran New Amsterdam. When the last governor of New Sweden, Johan Rising, tried to take over a Dutch outpost at Fort Casimir (now New Castle, Delaware), Stuyvesant sent hundreds of soldiers to force their surrender. They also took over New Sweden itself. In 1664, the Dutch would give up New Amsterdam to the British, who would rename it New York.

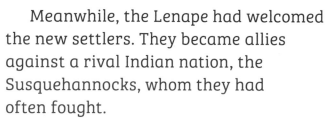

Meanwhile, the Lenape had welcomed the new settlers. They became allies against a rival Indian nation, the Susquehannocks, whom they had often fought.

In the many generations since that time, Philly, as it is known both to residents and outsiders, has become world-famous for its history, food, sports teams and fans, and musical traditions. People also love Philadelphia for its unique and interesting neighborhoods. In these areas, immigrants and other newcomers have built new lives. Some of the names reflect the pride of longtime Philadelphians for their heritage, like Germantown, Chinatown, and Bella Vista (Italian for "beautiful sight"). Other places reveal their history through their names, too—such as Fishtown, The Navy Yard, and Old City.

A Lenape woman in traditional clothing.

Philadelphians can also be proud of their city for its many firsts. In colonial times, it was the first "planned city," organized on a grid that included five big public squares. It also had America's first

The Pennsylvania Hospital houses America's first surgical amphitheater. There, students can watch surgeons operate on patients.

Elfreth's Alley features early American architecture in Philadelphia's Old City district.

public library (1731), founded by one of the city's most famous citizens, Benjamin Franklin. The Pennsylvania Hospital, opened in 1751, was the nation's first. The first volunteer fire department, the Union Fire Company, was also founded by Franklin, in 1736. The United States Mint opened in 1792 as the first producer of U.S. currency and coin. The list goes on and on, from the first municipal, or city, water system (1799) to America's first art museum, the Pennsylvania Academy of the Fine Arts. Meanwhile, Elfreth's Alley, which dates to 1703, is the nation's oldest continuously inhabited street.

The First Continental Congress, which met in Philly in 1774, set in motion the American Revolution. The city was the on-again-off-again capital of the Untited States until Washington, D.C., became the permanent one in 1790. While Philly is one of the best cities for taking in early American history, it is far more than a museum or colonial tourist destination. It is a living and breathing city of neighborhoods, each with its own unique accents, foods, traditions, and character.

This famous painting from 1772, *Penn's Treaty with the Indians*, commemorates an agreement reached between colonists and Native Americans in 1683. Top: England's King Charles II.

A City Like No Other

In 1681, King Charles II of England granted a charter to William Penn for over 45,000 square miles of land. This would become the colony, and later, state, of Pennsylvania. Penn was a Quaker, a member of a group of Christians who believe in nonviolence. Quakers also believe in living peacefully with and protecting other groups. They were important to the growth of both the colony and the state of Pennsylvania. Penn bought the land from the Lenape, and Pennsylvania was known for having better relations with Native Americans than the other American colonies.

Penn planned to build a major town on the Delaware River. He made that plan a reality when Philadelphia was founded on October 27, 1682. Its name is based loosely on the Greek words for "brotherly love." By 1701, a charter established it officially. The charter gave the mayor and other government officials the authority to run the city.

The city was laid out on a grid plan. Streets ran east-west and north-south between the Delaware and Schuylkill (SKOO-kul) rivers. Penn designed five public parks, too. Businesses and homes would be far apart, with gardens and other green spaces between them. This plan was designed partly to prevent fires. It got too crowded as more settlers arrived, however. Homeowners began dividing larger homes and buildings into smaller ones, providing more room for the many people flocking to the city.

If Philadelphia is "a city of neighborhoods," as many people call it, Old City is truly its first neighborhood. It was the first district built up after Penn established the town. By the mid-1700s, it was a busy area, with paved streets lined with oil-fueled street lamps. It was also a port. It shipped out many items, especially wood and other raw materials, to the Old World. Then it brought in finished products, such as fabric, for the colonists. Tradesmen also imported and sold indigo (an expensive blue dye used in clothing) and tea.

Philadelphia was a major center of shipbuilding and sailmaking, smithing (making metal products), shoemaking, rope making, and other skilled crafts. It also became famous for its clockmaking. This craft thrived when thousands of settlers, many of them highly skilled, arrived from Ireland, Switzerland, Germany, and other places.

Many of these products were sent or sold not just to England, but also to England's colonies in the Caribbean Sea and elsewhere, and throughout the other Thirteen Colonies. All this activity made Philadelphia among the most important cities in the northern colonies, alongside New York and Boston.

Newcomers joined the original Swedish, Dutch, and Germans of the colonial era. By the time of

The Philadelphia waterfront of the colonial era was a busy port.

the Revolution, Philadelphia's population was about 25 percent English, 30 percent Scots-Irish (from Scotland and Ireland), and 33 percent German.[1] French, Dutch, Welsh, and Swedish citizens also lived there.

This meeting house was built by the Free Quakers in 1783. Betsy Ross, credited with designing the American flag, was a member.

Some of the most important leaders and people in the city were English Quakers, but other Protestant and Catholic groups moved in as well. The Native Americans, who rarely lived in the city, moved farther west as many poorer immigrants, especially the Irish, took over the areas near the edges of the city. Until 1780, when Pennsylvania was the first state to outlaw slavery, both slaves and black freemen were a small minority in the city. Of white citizens, English Quakers and Germans opposed slavery most fiercely.

Other industries began to arise. Philadelphia's first paper mill was built in 1690, only a few years after the town's first printing press began running. In 1698, Francis Pastorius published one of the first school books in the colonies. Many of the other first publications were Quaker religious texts. William Bradford, Philadelphia's first printer, actually left town after he upset the Quakers with writings criticizing them. But his son, Andrew, returned in 1712 to establish the city's first independent press. He launched *The American Weekly Mercury* in 1719, Philadelphia's first newspaper.

Top: Ben Franklin works a printing press.

Bottom: Independence National Historical Park includes the Liberty Bell (inset) and Independence Hall. During record years, more than five million people have visited the park.

The City of Brotherly Love Grows

As the 18th century was ending, Philly became a key city for the American Revolution in the fight against England. It is where the Founding Fathers met to sign the Declaration of Independence in 1776. They also wrote the U.S. Constitution there, the legal plan for how the new government would run.

The Declaration was read on July 8, 1776, four days after its adoption. The Liberty Bell at the Pennsylvania State House (later known as Independence Hall) rang in celebration. In 1777, at the height of the Revolution, leaders worried that the British Army would capture the bell and melt it for ammunition. Rebel soldiers took it from the State House and hid it in a church basement in nearby Allentown. It was there for nearly a year before it was returned.

One of the most interesting, gifted, and beloved of the Founding Fathers was a man who moved from Boston to Philadelphia in 1723, at the age of seventeen: Benjamin Franklin. He owned his own press by 1728, and put out witty texts that made him one of the most popular writers in the colonies. In 1742, he became the first American printer to publish a novel: *Pamela* by Samuel Richardson. Unforunately, novels were popular in England, but sold poorly in the colonies. The publishing industry would continue to grow tremendously, however, from about 70,000 books printed

Franklin flies a kite in a thunderstorm. Using this experiment, he invented lightning rods, which prevented building fires.

Franklin's dedication to knowledge lives on in the Franklin Institute, a museum that has long promoted research and education on the physical sciences.

in Philadelphia in 1800 to nearly half a million by 1820.[1]

With his amazing knowledge on many subjects, Franklin co-founded the American Philosophical Society in 1743. It was one of several organizations that made the city a leader in America for science and medicine. His famous experiment, in which he flew a kite in a thunderstorm and demonstrated that lightning was an electrical charge, was one of just dozens of examples of his quest to understand how the world worked.

Mathew Carey was a pioneering immigrant publisher in the new nation, and he was a Philadelphian.

One immigrant from Ireland, Mathew Carey, met Franklin in Paris, France, in 1781. He became his protégé (or student). After immigrating to the United States in 1784, Carey helped make publishing better by insisting on proofreading (checking books for mistakes before they were printed). He also improved distribution methods. In 1789, his press put out America's first Roman Catholic Bible.

According to the U.S. Census, by 1801, with the new nation just a few years old, Philadelphia had a population of about 41,000 people. Publishing was just one of many areas that put this city on the map.

Like other American cities, Philly soon experienced the Industrial Revolution. Its neighborhoods grew along with its factories. The Manayunk area, for example, about eight miles northwest of Old City, was a sleepy place along the Schuylkill River until the Flat Rock Dam was finished in 1818, creating power for new textile mills. Ten mills were built by 1828, drawing hundreds of new workers. People even

The Flat Rock Dam helped transform the Manayunk area of Philadelphia into a center for textile manufacturing.

Dock Street Market was Philadelphia's first farmers market. It provided new immigrants with needed items as well as jobs.

traveled from overseas when they heard about the new opportunities. Manayunk became a center of cotton production. Homes for workers multiplied with the new jobs.

With the industrial age came industrial-age problems. Low pay, pollution, and poor health from overcrowding and working tough jobs made many workers' neighborhoods tough to live in. Still, many such areas grew, and some workers achieved better pay in their industries.

English, Irish, Scots, and Germans flooded the factories and neighborhoods. They built schools and churches and improved the roads. As in other American cities, neighborhoods grew around these cultural centers. Kensington, known for its shipbuilding and later its iron and steel factories, was home to many English and Irish

Rowhouses in Philadelphia were tightly packed, making use of as much space as possible.

workers. Germantown drew Germans who worked in its tanneries and yarn and knitting mills. The Irish were a majority in Harrowgate, Fishtown, Northern Liberties, and other districts. Many Irish worked as bricklayers, and their work helped put up buildings, bridges, and railroads.

In many Philadelphia neighborhoods from the 19th century into the 20th, one of the most popular kinds of homes was the rowhouse. These homes are connected, each sharing common walls with its neighbors. Rowhouses were popular among the poor, middle class, and rich. They created room for more people in a crowded and growing city.

The massive growth of the city led lawmakers to pass the Act of Consolidation in 1854. This expanded and united Philadelphia's neighborhoods with suburban ones. From just two square miles, Philadelphia grew to nearly 130 square miles overnight. It was the nation's largest city in area until Chicago beat it in 1889.

By 1897, electric trolleys were swiftly replacing horse-drawn carts and carriages.

Top: The above-ground West Philadelphia train station being demolished in 1931 to make way for a new one.

Middle: The new 30th Street Station kept trains underground.

Bottom: The Benjamin Franklin Parkway begins at LOVE Park, home of Robert Indiana's iconic *LOVE* statue.

Rising High

Philadelphia would expand and change in big ways—in population and size—throughout the later 19th century into the 20th. From the 1860s on, the city's older immigrant groups were joined by newer waves from Italy, Russia, and Eastern Europe.

African Americans also played a big role in the city's growth. Philly had the largest black population for a city in a non-slave state before the Civil War. After the war, even more former slaves and freemen arrived. As many as 32,000 African Americans lived there by 1880, rising to 63,000 by 1900.

When World War I erupted in 1914, the big flow of immigrants from Europe halted. More black workers flocked from the South to Philly to fill the jobs, just as the Irish and others had before them. This doubled the city's black population to 134,000 by 1920.[1] African Americans helped fill jobs in the steel mills, railroads, shipyards, and commuter rail network, the Philadelphia Rapid Transit Company. They also helped build 30th Street Station. Opened in 1933, the new railroad station in the University City neighborhood helped ease the train traffic at the old Broad Street station.

All hands on deck were needed as Philadelphia entered the modern era, with new buildings to show for it. The Pennsylvania Academy of the Fine Arts opened its new building in 1876. Many people compare its unique look to a jewel box. It was designed by Frank Furness, a Philly native who designed hundreds of buildings

The Academy of Fine Arts.

in and around the city. Furness was inspired by the city's industrial boom. He used steel and iron inside, skylights (new for their time), and colorful stonework outside. The Academy is still a working gallery with art studios today.

A world-class city also needs a world-class city hall. Taking 30 years to complete, Philadelphia City Hall certainly qualified when it opened in 1901. This beautiful and impressive building was designed by Scottish-born John McArthur, Jr., and American Thomas Ustick Walter. It is supported by walls of granite and brick, some as thick as 22 feet. It was the tallest non-church building in the world from 1894 until 1908, and remained Pennsylvania's tallest until 1932. In Philadelphia, it was the tallest until 1986, when the skyscraper complex at Liberty Place, at 58 stories and 848 feet, replaced it. There was even an unofficial agreement among builders and city officials for years not to build anything taller than City Hall. It also remains the largest municipal (city government) building in the world by area, with almost 700 rooms and 14.5 acres of floor space.

Philadelphians can be proud not only of their buildings, but also of their Ivy League school, the University of Pennsylvania. Founded in 1740 by Ben Franklin, UPenn boasts America's first business college (the Wharton School) and its first medical school (the Perelman School of Medicine). Its architectural program, now called PennDesign, is one of the best anywhere. The first computer, the Electronic Numerical Integrator and Computer (ENIAC), was developed at Penn, too. First used in 1946, the 30-ton computer did calculations in a 50-foot-long basement room.

Philadelphia City Hall, topped by a statue of William Penn.

The University of Pennsylvania is also well-known for its law school, Penn Carey Law.

Julian Abele, the first African American graduate of Penn's architecture program (finishing in 1902), went on to design hundreds of area buildings and institutions, including the Philadelphia Museum of Art. The

The Cathedral Basilica of Saints Peter and Paul has hosted two papal Masses in its history.

museum marks the endpoint of the Benjamin Franklin Parkway, which cuts through the city's main street grid. In 2017, workers broke ground on a three-year, $196 million project to fix and improve the museum.[2]

Other museums, city buildings, and schools dot the Parkway.

There's the Free Library of Philadelphia's Parkway Central Library, which was also designed by Julan Abele. It houses rare books and works of art. The Parkway's Cathedral Basilica of Saints Peter and Paul is the largest Catholic church in Pennsylvania and holds some of its Masses in Spanish. There's also The Rodin Museum, where you can see one of the largest collections of Rodin sculptures outside of Paris.

Also lining the Parkway are the flags of more than 100 countries. In 2010, when nineteen new flags were added along the Parkway, Mayor Michael Nutter said that the flags were a source of pride. "This is a city that was built by immigrants," he said.[3]

The Philadelphia Museum of Art is often featured in movies and television series.

The flags along the Benjamin Franklin Parkway were originally added as part of the city's bicentennial celebration.

Left: A trolley coasts along a Philadelphia street.

Below: The colorful lights of Geno's Steaks brighten the night in South Philadelphia.

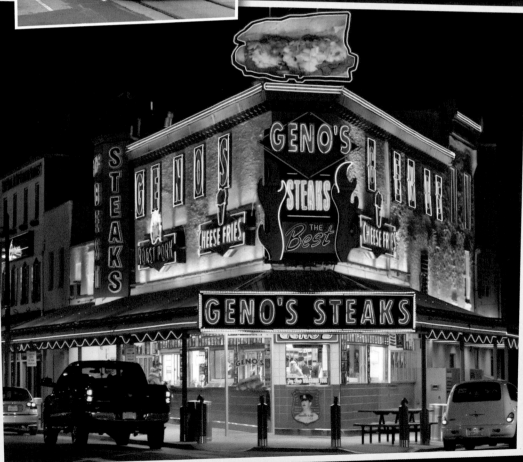

Philadelphia
Then and Now

Philadelphia has continued to be one of America's most interesting major cities. It has experienced great change, but it also has stayed a city of neighborhoods, immigrants, and proud residents. Tourists, businesspeople, and people seeking work continue to arrive in Philly every day.

Wherever they need to go, they can count on the Southeastern Pennsylvania Transportation Authority (SEPTA) to take them there. Launched in 1964, the state-owned network runs buses, trolleys, trains, and railroads in Philly and its suburbs. In one year riders made more than 326 million trips, on about 450 miles of train tracks and 1,400 buses.[1] SEPTA also runs trolleybuses, which are like regular buses but are powered by overhead cables.

Even if you know little about Philadelphia, you have probably heard of the town's signature meal: the Philly cheesesteak, a sandwich with hot sliced steak and melted cheese. Travel into South Philadelphia, still mostly an Italian neighborhood, and you will find the famous Italian Market, a ten-block stretch on South 9th Street. There, thousands annually visit Pat's King of Steaks, whose owner Pat Olivieri invented the cheesesteak in 1930 with his brother Harry. Directly across the street is its main competitor, Geno's Steaks, founded in 1966. The many vendors in the Italian Market have been joined in recent years by Mexican, Vietnamese, Korean, Thai, Chinese, Laotian, and other vendors from around the world.

Citizens Bank Park, home of the Philadelphia Phillies, used 450,000 handlaid bricks to create an old-time ballpark feel.

Another major draw in this area is the South Philadelphia Sports Complex. It houses the Wells Fargo Center, home of the National Hockey League's Philadelphia Flyers and the National Basketball Association's Philadelphia 76ers. Home base for the Philadelphia Phillies Major League Baseball franchise is there, too, at Citizens Bank Park. Nearby, the

Lincoln Financial Field, home of the Philadelphia Eagles, features wind vanes that help power the stadium.

Philadelphia is well-known for its stunning historical murals.

Philadelphia Eagles, the city's National Football League team, plays at Lincoln Financial Field. Philadelphians celebrated wildly in 2018 when the Eagles took home their very first Super Bowl trophy.

The city's museums and other sites are just part of Philadelphia's artistic and cultural heritage. One form of public art that allows residents to express themselves is the mural. These are large paintings that cover building walls and other surfaces. Murals have been part of the city for generations. Older ones from the nineteenth century are mostly gone. Newer ones include those that were paid for by the Federal Art Project, started in 1935. In the 1970s, a community art movement sparked more than 150 new murals. In the last couple of decades, muralists have tackled politics, immigrant and civil rights, and Philadelphia history.

Music is another way that Philadelphia shines. The Musical Fund Society started in 1820 and paved the way for the Philadelphia Orchestra, one of the most respected classical music institutions in

The 2,500-seat Verizon Hall is part of the Kimmel Center for the Performing Arts in Philly's Center City district.

the world. Philly has also been influential in many African American musical forms. Jazz legends Dizzy Gillespie and John Coltrane both called the city home.

The city was also one of several important sources of doo-wop music, popular in the 1950s and early 1960s. Several pop and rock and roll legends are also from Philly, including Frankie Avalon, Fabian, and Bill Haley. Later, rhythm and blues and a genre known as Philly Soul made their mark in the 1960s and 1970s. Groups and artists in this local genre include Chubby Checker, Patti LaBelle, the Spinners, the Delfonics, and the O'Jays. These paved the way for later groups like the Four Tops and Hall & Oates. Beanie Sigel, named after Sigel Street in South Philadelphia, the Roots, vocalist Meek Mill, and rap pioneer

The Academy of Music in Philadelphia is the oldest opera house in the U.S. still used as an opera house.

Schooly D all represent the city. One of the most successful rap groups was DJ Jazzy Jeff & the Fresh Prince. They sold millions of records in the 1990s before the group's vocalist, Will Smith, a West Philadelphia native, became a world-famous television and movie star.

Yet another Philly tradition that lives on is the annual Mummers Parade, which takes place each year on New Year's Day. Groups known as New Years Associations march and perform. They compete

Costumed mummers take to Philly's streets annually on New Year's Day.

A nighttime view of Philly's skyline is a reminder of how beautiful a city can be.

against each other with incredible costumes, comedy routines, string band performances, and artworks. Working-class people started the parades and mummers clubs in the 17th century. (The official parade began in 1901.) The mummery stems from British and Irish roots, combined with Finnish and Swedish Christmas traditions.[2]

Philly continues to grow and change. Many of its old industrial neighborhoods no longer have factories. Instead, fancy apartments, night clubs, lively restaurants, and other service businesses have

Market Street has always been central to Philadelphia life.

begun to appear. Some areas have grown richer, and many residents fear that as they do, older residents and their children might be pushed out.

Nevertheless, Philadelphians still feel a pride and fighting spirit. At the bottom of the 72 steps leading up to the Philadelphia Museum of Art stands a bronze statue based on the lead character from the 1976 film *Rocky*. In the film, an underdog working-class boxer, the Italian American Rocky Balboa, jogs to the top of the stairs as fans chase and cheer him on. Many city residents feel the statue is a fitting symbol of the city of neighborhoods and brotherly love.

The Rocky statue, arms raised in triumph.

Chronology

Pre-colonial times   The Lenape live in the area that will become Pennsylvania.

1638   Swedish settlers land in the Delaware River Valley near modern Philadelphia. They start the colony of New Sweden.

1655   The Dutch conquer New Sweden.

1681   England's King Charles II gives the land of future Pennsylvania to William Penn.

1682   Philadelphia is founded.

1701   An official city charter sets up the government of Philadelphia.

1719   Andrew Bradford begins publishing Philadelphia's first newspaper, *The American Weekly Mercury*.

1723   Benjamin Franklin arrives in the city from Boston. He begins his career as a printer, statesman, inventor, and Founding Father.

1740   Franklin establishes the University of Pennsylvania.

1776   At the Pennsylvania State House (later known as Independence Hall), the Liberty Bell rings to celebrate the signing of the Declaration of Independence.

1805   The Pennsylvania Academy of the Fine Arts is founded.

1818   The Flat Rock Dam is built on the Schuylkill River, making it possible to build mills. The new jobs attract workers from all over the United States and Europe.

1854   The Act of Consolidation combines central Philadelphia with surrounding areas. It makes the city the largest by area in the United States.

1876   The current building for the Pennsylvania Academy of the Fine Arts opens. It is designed by Frank Furness and George W. Hewitt. The Philadelphia Museum of Art is founded.

1901   After years of construction, Philadelphia City Hall opens.

1930   The Olivieri brothers invent the Philly cheesesteak. Pat Olivieri opens Pat's King of Steaks in South Philadelphia.

1946   The University of Pennsylvania begins using ENIAC, the world's first modern computer.

1966   A competitor to Pat's, Geno's, opens across from Pat's. This intersection becomes known as Cheesesteak Corner.

1976   The film *Rocky* is released. It becomes an important part of Philadelphia pop culture and mythology.

1986   One Liberty Place becomes the tallest structure in the city. At 945 feet tall, it surpasses City Hall.

2008   Comcast Center takes the title of tallest building in Philadelphia.

Glossary

architect (AR-kih-tekt)—A person who designs houses, apartments, and other buildings and structures.

charter (CHAR-ter)—An official document that gives the power and permission to govern a school, city, town, or other group of people.

colony (KAH-luh-nee)—A group of people from another place that continues to be governed by the first place.

complex (KOM-pleks)—A group of buildings that hold related businesses.

Founding Fathers—The group of powerful people in the American colonies who began a rebellion against British rule. They created the Declaration of Independence and the U.S. Constitution.

freemen—Black citizens of the United States who were born free, or who had been released from slavery.

grid—A plan for a city or town in which the streets run at right angles to each other.

inhabit (in-HAB-it)—To live within a building, such as a house or apartment, or a place, such as a city or town.

mummers (MUH-mers)—People in costumes who gather to celebrate yearly in Philadelphia on New Year's Day.

municipal (myoo-NIH-sih-pul)—Handled or controlled by the city or city government.

Philly cheesesteak (CHEEZ-stayk)—A popular, Philly-born, fast-food sandwich consisting of hot shaved steak and melted cheese stuffed into a soft sub roll.

proofreading (PROOF-ree-ding)—Checking for mistakes in books, magazines, and other written materials.

Quakers (KWAY-kers)—Members of a Christian group known as the Religious Society of Friends. They believe in accepting and living peacefully with many different groups and religions.

Scandinavian (skan-dih-NAY-vee-in)—From Scandinavia, the area of Europe that includes the countries of Norway, Sweden, Finland, Denmark, and Iceland.

trolleybus (TRAH-lee-bus)—A kind of bus that runs on rails and is powered not by an engine, but by overhead electrical wires.

Index